THE CHRISTIAN RESPONSE

I WAS HUNGRY!

DOUGLAS ARTHUR AND DOUGLAS JACOBY

I Was Hungry! *The Christian Response to Poverty*

This is a revised edition of the 1987 original version.

© 2022 by Douglas Arthur and Douglas Jacoby

ISBN:978-1-953623-80-5. Printed in the United States of America.

Unless otherwise indicated, all Scripture references are from the **Holy Bible, New International Version,** copyright ©1973, 1978, 1984, 2011 by Biblica, Inc. Used by permission. All rights reserved worldwide.

Interior layout: Toney Mulhollan. Cover design: Roy Appalsamy.

Dr. Douglas Jacoby is a freelance teacher and consultant. With degrees from Duke, Harvard, and Drew, he has written more than thirty books, recorded over 1000 podcasts, and spoken in 125 nations around the world. Douglas is also a professor of Bible and Theology at Lincoln Christian University and professor of Bible and Apologetics at the Rocky Mountain School of Ministry and Theology. Douglas and his wife, Vicki, live in Scotland. For more information about Douglas Jacoby, see his website, www.DouglasJacoby.com.

Douglas Arthur now serves as the Global Missions Director for the Beam Missions Foundation. In 1981, Douglas married Joyce, and together with six others, they planted a church in London, England. Ten years later, God multiplied the faith of 8 to be a congregation of more than a thousand disciples. Later they would lead dynamic congregations in Washington DC and Boston, Massachusetts. Currently, Douglas is focused on a global network of training centers that train next-generation leaders worldwide. You can learn more at www.Beammissions.org.

ILLUMINATION PUBLISHERS www.ipibooks.com

Contents

Foreword to the Second Edition

This reprinting is a testimony to the responsive hearts of our fellowship. We are part of the "Restoration Movement," which has a long history of seeking to find God's will in his inspired Word. When we discover it, we strive to put it into practice. That is precisely what happened some 35 years ago with our family. This book was first published in 1987. It was a time when we began to wrestle, individually and collectively, with God's word related to our responsibility in taking care of those less fortunate than ourselves.

Douglas and Douglas were both in their mid-twenties and on a missionary journey together to London, England. What was unique about this story is that it neither started nor ended with us. Young disciples reading their Bibles in London began to ask questions like, "Why we didn't talk about the poor much, and why don't we have a plan to help?" These awkward yet straightforward questions stirred us to dig deep in our Bibles to find the answers. The answers were hard to miss because the Bible was covered with directives about the poor. Our convictions grew, and our compassion did too.

The Gospel was spreading rapidly in London, and soon plans were underway to send a mission team to India. Our convictions solidified in our hearts on that Indian "scouting trip" to Calcutta, Chennai, and eventually Bangalore. We knew that we needed to change, and we needed to invite our brothers and sisters to join us in our repentance. It was that resolve that led me to take the opportunity to preach a message entitled "Born of Water and the Spirit" at the World Missions seminar in 1987, in which I challenged the entire fellowship from the scriptures to respond and "love the poor even more" like Jesus did.

Thousands responded and began the story of the LOVE offering, which evolved into what we now know as HOPE *worldwide.* Godly sorrow swept the fellowship, and we witnessed a fantastic display of what godly sorrow can produce. "Earnestness, eagerness, indignation, alarm, longing, concern, and a readiness to see justice done" were all evident worldwide.

In the next few decades, hundreds of orphans were adopted into loving homes, thousands were healed of leprosy, tens of thousands were immunized or treated for HIV, and millions were given lifegiving medical attention —for free! Hundreds of millions of dollars have been given to help the poor worldwide. This all happened because our families of churches chose to go back to the Bible, listen to what it said, and "prove our repentance by our deeds."

Thousands of disciples are again gathering, this time in Orlando, Florida. This small book was provided to every participant by HOPE *worldwide* for two main reasons. The first is to remind us of our calling and biblical convictions to love the poor. The second is to remind us of God's actions in just a few years. Let's use this time to marvel together at all he has done and dream about even greater things in the years to come.

—Douglas Arthur

The Christian Response to Poverty

In our efforts to restore New Testament Christianity it is appropriate that we now turn our attention to a topic that has captured the hearts of more and more Christians the world over: the necessity of meeting the needs of the poor, as Jesus did.

This whole subject of the Christian response to poverty is, we must admit, an area in which we have vacillated quite a bit in the past few years. If you are like us, you may even have made mutually contradictory statements about the Christian response to poverty.

Why all the vacillation? For one, there is a lack of knowledge about the needs, worldwide. Also, there isn't consistent teaching on the subject. Preachers whom we have talked to tend to change their positions frequently. Moreover, this is not a topic normally assigned in Christian seminars or conferences or Zoom meetings. Furthermore, it is easy to grow tired of talk about money: benevolence, regular Sunday contributions, missions, and so on. As a result, while Christians hold their own private views on poverty, they are often not convinced that there exists a consistent scriptural doctrine on the issue.

Both reading and experience can play vital roles in helping you to solidify your own opinions on giving to the poor, and many volumes have been written on the subject. As for experience, poverty is present the world over, and it should not be too difficult—especially in these days of televised starvation and poverty—to develop a feel for the world situation. Ultimately, however, it is God's word that is the authority on the subject.

Our conviction was crystallized after a scouting visit to India in December 1985. We began in Calcutta, a city of 14 million—the largest in India—built to accommodate only one million. Calcutta is the city where Mother Teresa ministered to the hundreds who live and die on its streets every day. Indeed, acute poverty and squalor are shocking to Western eyes, and we spent most of that first night in India deep in sobered thought.

Our prayer is not that you will agree with everything we say. Our prayer is that you will allow God's word to transform your thinking about poverty. That is bound to happen as we are transformed into the likeness of Christ, who, though rich, for our sakes became poor.

I. When You Give to the Needy

Seven years ago, we were exposed to a biblical truth. Although we were vaguely familiar with this truth, we had never practiced it. The topic was fasting, and the teacher was Albert Lemmons. Two of his most compelling points were (a) "There are more references in the Scriptures to fasting than there are to repentance, baptism, and the Lord's Supper combined," and (b) *"Jesus said, 'When you pray....'"*—assuming that we would all be praying. But he also said, *'When you fast....'* Obviously, he was also assuming that we would be fasting." Since that night, biblical fasting has become a consistent part of our Christian lives.

In our personal study on giving to the poor, we were startled by two realities: (a) The poor and the needy are mentioned three times as often as fasting, and (b) Jesus began his discourse in Matthew 6 with *"When you give to the needy...."* Once again Jesus' obvious assumption is that we would be giving to the needy *regularly.*

Individual Per Capita Income

Afghanistan	$490
Chad	$524
Sudan	$553
Ethiopia	$744
Haiti	$1,201
Nigeria	$1,779
India	$1,822
Vietnam	$2,163
The Philippines	$3,472
South Africa	$4,862
Jamaica	$5,040
Turkey	$7,585
Brazil	$7,629
Mexico	$7,750
Argentina	$8,162
China	$8,334
Russian Federation	$8,940
Poland	$13,255
United Kingdom	$35,835
United Arab Emirates	$39,306
Australia	$42,151
The Netherlands	$43,778
Singapore	$48,344
United States	$55,419
Switzerland	$65,600

According to The World Bank, 2019

II. Yesterday, Today, and Forever

As far back as the law of Moses, God has *always* insisted that his people be actively involved in helping the poor. In this section we will make a survey of the major divisions of Scripture, showing that Jesus' assumption in Matthew 6 was nothing new or unfounded, but rather rooted in the entire revelation of God to mankind. For the sake of brevity, we will examine only one book in each division of Scripture.

Law

The books of the Law (torah) contain scores of references to taking care of the poor. Although it is probably the book of Leviticus that contains the strongest teaching on taking care of the needy (especially Chapter 25, with its radical economics),we will turn our attention to Deuteronomy 15:4-5,11:

> *However, there should be no poor among you, for in the land the Lord your God is giving you to possess as your inheritance, he will richly bless you, if only you fully obey the Lord your God....*

> *There will always be poor people in the land. Therefore, I command you to be open-handed towards your brothers and toward the poor and needy in your land.*

In a paradox, the Lord says to the people of Israel that there *should* be no poor people in the land, but that there *always will* be. Why is this? Firstly, the promise was conditional on Israel's obedience, and, secondly, we believe that God knew that many Israelites would not care for their neighbors, thus ensuring that there was a continuing number of the needy to help. (Jesus made a similar statement in Matthew 26:11, Mark 14:7, John 12:8.)

Moreover, we notice that the concern for the poor upon which God insisted was to extend beyond the borders of their "fellowship." As usual, God only calls us to be like him:

> *(God) defends the cause of the fatherless and the widow, and loves the alien, giving him food and clothing* (Deuteronomy 10:18).

Thus, we see that in the Law of Moses God insists that his people be actively involved in helping the poor.

Prophets

There are many passages in the prophetic literature on the topic of meeting the needs of the poor, and in many places doing so is virtually equated with righteousness (Jeremiah 22:16). Consider Isaiah 58:6-10 on "True Fasting."

"Is not this the kind of fasting I have chosen: to loosen the chains of injustice and untie the cords of the yoke, to set the oppressed free and break every yoke?

Is it not to share your food with the hungry and to provide the poor wanderer with shelter—when you see the naked, to clothe him, and not to turn away from your own flesh and blood?

Then your light will break forth like the dawn, and your healing will quickly appear, then your righteousness will go before you, and the glory of the Lord will be your rear guard. Then you will call, and the Lord will answer; you will cry for help, and he will say: Here am I.

If you do away with the yoke of oppression, with the pointing finger and malicious talk, and if you spend yourselves on behalf of the hungry and satisfy the needs of the oppressed, then your light will rise in the darkness, and your night will become like the noonday. " (Isaiah 58:6-10).

Going through the motions of religion without a sincere effort to meet the needs of our fellow human beings is worthless. There is quite a difference between fasting and true fasting, between religion and true religion (James 1:27). Yet how many of us can say that we "spend ourselves on behalf of the hungry," except for ourselves when we are hungry?

All the prophets testify together with Isaiah that social concern is not merely a peripheral concern for the man or woman of God. It is central. The second division of the Old Testament joins with the first to insist that God's people truly care for the poor.

Writings

The writings, the third and final division of the Hebrew scriptures, also agree that our treatment of the poor is a good test of our character, and a major part of righteousness. One can hardly read passages like Job 24:1-12 and 31:16-23 without getting the point, and there are many passages, especially in the Wisdom Literature, that touch on our theme. Let us consider some of the Proverbs:

He who oppresses the poor shows contempt for their Maker, but whoever is kind to the needy honors God (14:31).

He who is kind to the poor lends to the Lord, and he will reward him for what he has done (19:17).

In these proverbs we learn that the way we treat the poor is the way we are treating God— at the very least a stingy heart is culpable. It is hardly to one's credit when one does not actively oppress the poor; the "Golden Rule" (Matthew 7:12) must come into play. Is this not the same lesson Jesus so forcefully taught in Matthew 25:31-46 (The Parable of the Sheep and the Goats)? Proverbs 28:27 reads:

He who gives to the poor will lack nothing, but he who closes his eyes to them receives many curses.

How often we *would* give to the poor, but are afraid that if we do so some of our "needs" may go unmet? Surely the Lord who bade us trust him for the necessities of life (Matthew 6:25-34) will not let us down when we step out on faith and open our arms to our neighbors in need.

As the Proverbs state, we can give to the poor and still lack nothing. Moreover, giving is a reflective action: surely part of giving being more blessed than receiving is the blessing which accrues when we give. This blessing may be no more than peace of mind and assurance that we are taking God at his word, yet often it is far more than that. See Proverbs 11:17, 24, 25; 14:21; 22:9.

Materialism is no less a threat to our churches today than it was to the Laodicean community. One of the most useful proverbs addressing the need for moderation is Proverbs 30:7-9:

"Two things I ask of you, O Lord;
   do not refuse me before I die:
Keep falsehood and lies far from me;
   give me neither poverty nor riches,
   but give me only my daily bread.
Otherwise, I may have too much and disown you
   and say, 'Who is the Lord?'
Or I may become poor and steal,
   and so dishonor the name of my God."

Materialism cannot, however, be defined as having more than the necessities when there are others in need.

The "wife of noble character" is commended for her generosity to the poor (Proverbs 31:20) even while she is clothed in fine linen and purple (Proverbs 31:22). There is no inherent virtue in poverty, and certainly none in asceticism.

It would appear God is asking us to do more than just contribute to our favorite charity; he is looking for some positive action:

"Speak up for those who cannot speak for themselves, and for the rights of all who are destitute.
Speak up and judge fairly; defend the rights of the poor and needy" (31:8,9).

And what is God's assessment of our character if we cannot be bothered to think of our fellow humans with kind compassion and concern? Proverbs 29:7:

The righteous care about justice for the poor,
but the wicked have no such concern.

Perhaps we have considered making some changes in our lifestyle or giving habits. We are warned in Proverbs 3:27-28:

Do not withhold good from those who deserve it,
  when it is in your power to act.
Do not say to your neighbor, "Come back later;
  I'll give it tomorrow"—
  when you now have it with you.

Granted, we are instructed to give to those who deserve it—indiscriminate giving can be a waste of the Lord's money—but most of us could do a lot more to meet the needs of others than we are doing.

Finally, consider one of the most haunting verses in Proverbs, namely Proverbs 21:13:

If a man shuts his ears to the cry of the poor, he too will cry out and not be answered.

Consider the following Literacy Rates in select countries in 2018:

- Sudan **31%**
- Ethiopia **39%**
- Liberia **43%**
- Haiti **49%**
- Nigeria **51%**
- Pakistan **55%**
- India **69%**
- Egypt **72%**
- United States **88%**
- Brazil **90%**
- South Africa **93%**
- Mexico **93%**
- Finland **100%**

Gospels

Although most Christians are far more familiar with the Gospels than they are with the Old Testament, the strong emphasis on concern for the poor is as overlooked here as it is in the Old Testament. Let us center on the Gospel of Luke as we continue our overview of the scriptural teaching on how disciples of Jesus should react to poverty. In all, we have found some 31 passages in this gospel which touch on our subject. Luke 3:10, 11:

"What should we do then?" the crowd asked. John answered, "The man with two tunics should share with him who has none, and the one who has food should do the same."

As John the Baptist prepares the ground for Jesus' ministry, he calls the people to selfless sharing and economic contentment. In fact, all three of John's practicals concerning repentance as recorded by Luke concern economic matters: sharing food and clothes, refraining from fraud and extortion, and being content with our pay. How many of us would have felt comfortable being baptized by John? Carefully read Luke 6:20b, 24-25a):

"Blessed are you who are poor, for yours is the kingdom of God...But woe to you who are rich, for you have already received your comfort. Woe to you who are well fed now, for you will go hungry."

Who are these "rich" whom Jesus condemns? Can we safely assume that the only rich Jesus had in mind were the oppressors of James 5:1-6? Certainly, it is no easy thing for the rich to enter the kingdom of heaven (Luke 18:24, Deuteronomy 17:17), but it is indisputable that there were rich people in the early church. They were commanded to put their hope in God rather than in their wealth, and to generously share with others that with which God had blessed them (1 Timothy 6:17,18). Thus, a broad understanding of the word of God does not lead us to the conclusion that Jesus taught in the Sermon that it is a sin to be rich. As in the Sermon on the Mount (Matthew 5-7), it is the inward orientation of the heart that is at issue. However, it is simply not true that the admonitions of Luke 6 can be spiritualized to mean the same thing as those in Matthew 5. Jesus is discussing economic matters in Luke 6:30,31:

> *"Give to everyone who asks you, and if anyone takes what belongs to you, do not demand it back. Do to others as you would have them do to you."*

Is it surprising to you that the "Golden Rule" is embedded in such a context? Generosity, particularly with our money and possessions, is required by our merciful father. Does this mean that we should encourage people to take advantage of us, to borrow without repayment? No, this is no license to borrow without repaying; *"The wicked borrow and do not repay..."* (Psalm 37:21) and (*"The Most High) is kind to the ungrateful and wicked"* (Luke 6:35). Jesus is here concerned with our attitude towards material things. *"Why not rather be wronged? Why not rather be cheated?"* (1 Corinthians 6:7). The open heart is a giving heart, and because it understands that it is only an unworthy steward it does not *demand* any reward or repayment, although it may hope for such. Sometimes someone is not able to repay us; what is our attitude at such times? The parable of the unmerciful servant comes to mind (Matthew 18:21-35).

Luke 10:25-37 tells of the Parable of the Good Samaritan:

On one occasion an expert in the law stood up to test Jesus. "Teacher," he asked, "what must I do to inherit eternal life?"

"What is written in the Law?" he replied. "How do you read it?"

He answered, "'Love the Lord your God with all your heart and with all your soul and with all your strength and with all your mind'; and, 'Love your neighbor as yourself.'"

"You have answered correctly," Jesus replied. "Do this and you will live."

But he wanted to justify himself, so he asked Jesus, "And who is my neighbor?"

In reply Jesus said: "A man was going down from Jerusalem to Jericho, when he was attacked by robbers. They stripped him of his clothes, beat him and went away, leaving him half dead. A priest happened to be going down the same road, and when he saw the man, he passed by on the other side. So too, a Levite, when he came to the place and saw him, passed by on the other side. But a Samaritan, as he traveled, came where the man was; and when he saw him, he took pity on him. He went to him and bandaged his wounds, pouring on oil and wine. Then he put the man on his own donkey, brought him to an inn and took care of him. The next day he took out two denarii and gave them to the innkeeper. 'Look after him,' he said, 'and when I return, I will reimburse you for any extra expense you may have.'

"Which of these three do you think was a neighbor to the man who fell into the hands of robbers?"

The expert in the law replied, "The one who had mercy on him."

Often this passage is used to exhort us to evangelize, and rightly so, since meeting the needs of strangers is Jesus' whole point in the parable. But taken at face value this contains a plethora of principles on meeting the needs of the poor. What was the situation?

1. The "Good" Samaritan was aware of his need.

The unfortunate victim had something of a raw deal. So do millions in the world today: they were born into a situation of inequality, limited opportunity, poverty, decadence, etc. Through the mass media most of us are aware of their needs; we cannot plead ignorance. Neither could the priest and the Levite.

2. The race of the victim was irrelevant to the Good Samaritan.

Even though the victim was likely a Jew, the (half-breed) Samaritan hero did not let that prejudice his love for his neighbor. How many of us would react differently if the disadvantaged of the world belonged to our own comfortable social and racial set? Do differences in skin color and other outward features allow us to distance us from the world of human suffering and need?

3. Others were not meeting his needs.

The ones who had the least excuse, here representing respectable religion, actively went out of their way to avoid the pangs of conscience that might have led them to imitate the merciful God they claimed as their own.

4. The victim could not help himself.

He was in no position to help himself. He is probably not the person on welfare who could work but prefers not to. He is probably not the familiar Western tramp asking donations for alcohol. But there is a world out there of countless millions who are in legitimate need. Unless we help them, it is unlikely anyone will. The various relief organizations barely begin to meet their needs; no, we cannot excuse our inactivity with the rationalization that others are getting the job done.

This, then, is the situation. What does the Samaritan do?

1. He sees the need.
2. He takes pity on his neighbor. Let's not argue about who our neighbor is; every person is our neighbor!
3. He provides care and meets physical needs.
4. He gives money to a responsible agency (the innkeeper).
5. He does not limit his liability, but is willing to meet the need.

When it comes to meeting the needs of the world's poor, Jesus bids us, "Go and do likewise."

We now come to one of the most provocative commandments to Christians in general in the entire New Testament, for many of us more challenging than the command to repent and be baptized (Acts 2:38).

"Sell your possessions and give to the poor. Provide purses for yourselves that will not wear out, a treasure in heaven that will never fail, where no thief comes near and no moth destroys. For where your treasure is, there your heart will be also." (Luke 12:33-34).

This passage must be addressed uniquely to the Twelve Apostles. Christians are not asked to sell all their possessions, so this verse must apply only to the apostles. At least that's how we interpreted it for years, until we saw that to limit it to the Apostles meant limiting the admonition not to worry (v.22) and to seek his kingdom (v.31) to the apostles as well.

It is easy to overreact to challenging passages, reinterpreting their original context or even resorting to *reductio ad absurdum.* But the passage does not say that we have to sell all our possessions, any more than Jesus, when he says, *"When you give to the needy,"* expects us to give everything we own to the needy. The point of the passage is: (a) let your treasure be in heaven, and your heart will follow; (b) make selling your possessions and giving to the poor a regular feature of your life.

Luke 16:19-24 reads:

"There was a rich man who was dressed in purple and fine linen and lived in luxury every day. At his gate was laid a beggar named Lazarus, covered with sores and longing to eat what fell from the rich man's table. Even the dogs came and licked his sores.

"The time came when the beggar died and the angels carried him to Abraham's side. The rich man also died and was buried. In Hades, where he was in torment, he looked up and saw Abraham far away, with Lazarus by his side. So he called to him, 'Father Abraham, have pity on me and send Lazarus to dip the tip of his finger in water and cool my tongue, because I am in agony in this fire.'"

The poor of the world are at our gate. They are not saved *because* they are poor, any more than we are condemned *because* we are rich. Eternal reward and punishment are determined by one's relationship with God, not one's economic status. Lazarus is a worthy case. He had to be carried and apparently was not strong enough to prevent the dogs from licking his festering sores. How could the rich man live sumptuously while this needy case lay at his gate?

The irony is that Lazarus lay on the outside looking in, longing to trade places with the rich man's dogs, and now the rich man is on the outside looking in, longing for a drop of water.

So it will be with anyone who does not love his neighbor as himself. Is not this the message of Luke? His economic emphasis is not subtle; it is in the mainstream gospel.

The fact is that *all* the Gospels reveal God's attitude towards the poor and his desire that we love them as we do all people.

Acts

Did the early church take to heart the teaching of the Old Testament as well as the teachings of Jesus? The only way we know the answer is to go to the book of Acts and read 2:44-45 followed by 2:32-35.

All the believers were together and had everything in common. They sold property and possessions to give to anyone who had need.

"God has raised this Jesus to life, and we are all witnesses of it. Exalted to the right hand of God, he has received from the Father the promised Holy Spirit and has poured out what you now see and hear. For David did not ascend to heaven, and yet he said,

"'The Lord said to my Lord:
"Sit at my right hand
until I make your enemies
a footstool for your feet."'"

Yes, they did! Having "everything in common" is not to be understood as communism, for the rights to private property did not cease. Christians were never required to sell all they had; Again, the rich young ruler is the only one ever required to do that. Why? Although landowners (the wealthiest Christians; most did not own their own homes or land) took the lead in sharing their wealth—and rightly so—apparently, they were not compelled to surrender their property; this was purely at the discretion of individual disciples. There is no suggestion that those who chose not to were regarded as less "spiritual" by the community. This was not Christian socialism, since the church did not assume the right to lands and houses. Nor was economic equality the fundamental purpose of such sharing. Their *attitude,* however, could be described as communistic, since private property was abolished in their hearts: *"No one claimed that any of his possessions was his own."*

Notice that the apostles had the discretion to decide what would be done with the proceeds of the sales. Although individual Christians transacted the sales—church leaders are not in the real estate business—responsible leadership decided exactly what would be done with the money.

Finally, there were enough needy people within the church that the immediate financial generosity of the disciples did not extend beyond their fellowship; we are aware of the economic duress experienced by the early church. This in no way relieves us of our obligation to help our brothers and sisters overseas, in countries where poverty and injustice are facts of everyday life, or to obey the clear teaching on giving to the poor in other scriptures.

In Acts 6:7 we read:

So the word of God spread. The number of disciples in Jerusalem increased rapidly, and a large number of priests became obedient to the faith.

Instead of using this verse only to illustrate the rapid growth of the early church, let us see *why* the rapid growth continued. May it not be that the cause of the growth was the action taken to ensure social justice within the redeemed community of God? When concrete Christian love is displayed (1 John 3:16-18), hearts are touched. Rather than being a distraction and a threat to a multiplying ministry, this portion of God's word suggests that assisting the poor can be tremendously beneficial in stimulating evangelism and conversion. As the Lord said in John 13:35: *"By this everyone will know that you are my disciples, if you love one another."*

Luke 11:27-30 reads:

> *As Jesus was saying these things, a woman in the crowd called out, "Blessed is the mother who gave you birth and nursed you."*
>
> *He replied, "Blessed rather are those who hear the word of God and obey it."*
>
> *As the crowds increased, Jesus said, "This is a wicked generation. It asks for a sign, but none will be given it except the sign of Jonah. For as Jonah was a sign to the Ninevites, so also will the Son of Man be to this generation."*

The concern for others in the famine during the reign of Claudius (41-54 AD) is obvious. The disciples were moved to action, and each gave *"in keeping with his income."* We are not all expected to give in the same way (1 Corinthians 16:2), but we are all expected to give *something.* Some can give more than others.

In closing, lest one make the argument that early Christian giving was confined only to Christians, consider two selfless individuals, one a disciple and the other not even a member of the of the body of

Christ: Acts 9:36 reads:

> *"In Joppa there was a disciple named Tabitha...*
> *who was always doing good and helping the poor."*

Acts 10:1,2 and 4b reads:

> *At Caesarea there was a man named Corne-*
> *lius, a centurion in what was known as the Italian*
> *Regiment. He and all his family were devout and*
> *God-fearing; he gave generously to those in need*
> *and prayed to God regularly... The angel answered,*
> *"Your prayers and gifts to the poor have come up*
> *as a memorial offering before God."*

We are shamed in our giving to the poor by many "unknown soldiers" who give liberally without expectation of reward. Some of these are in our brotherhood. Sadly, most are outside the borders of spiritual Israel. Nonetheless, let us reach out to them as the Lord reached out to Cornelius.

The concern of the early church did not stop with the end of the first century. History records that by 250 AD in Rome some 1500 needy persons were receiving regular support from the church there (Martin Hengel, *Property and Riches in the Early Church,* pages

42-44). The church's social welfare programs contributed in large part to the early church's popularity even before the Edict of Toleration (c.312) and Christianity's becoming the official state religion (c.381). Julian the Apostate (emperor 361-363), who tried to return the Roman Empire to paganism, undoing the work of the previous "Christian" emperors, admitted that "the godless Galileans (our brothers and sisters) feed not only their poor but ours also." He was abashed that, whereas the pagans had utterly failed to assist the poor, the Christians gladly did so, even those poor who were not members of the church.

Letters

The letters abound with references to giving to the poor, but in our survey of the major divisions of Scripture we will limit ourselves to James.

James first approaches the rich/poor theme in James 1:9-11, but his major treatment of it is 2:1-17. Until recently, we had always separated this section into four:

- Favoritism forbidden (2:1-7)
- Loving your neighbor as yourself (2:8-11)
- Being merciful (2:12, 13), and
- Faith and deeds (2:14ff).

On closer examination we suggest you consider this analysis: James 2:1-13 deals with the rich/poor theme. Beginning in 2:14 faith and deeds is the topic. Read James 2:1-17:

My brothers and sisters, believers in our glorious Lord Jesus Christ must not show favoritism. Suppose a man comes into your meeting wearing a gold ring and fine clothes, and a poor man in filthy old clothes also comes in. If you show special attention to the man wearing fine clothes and say, "Here's a good seat for you," but say to the poor man, "You stand there" or "Sit on the floor by my feet," have you not discriminated among yourselves and become judges with evil thoughts?

Listen, my dear brothers and sisters: Has not God chosen those who are poor in the eyes of the world to be rich in faith and to inherit the kingdom he promised those who love him? But you have dishonored the poor. Is it not the rich who are exploiting you? Are they not the ones who are dragging you into court? Are they not the ones who are blaspheming the noble name of him to whom you belong?

If you really keep the royal law found in Scripture, "Love your neighbor as yourself," you are doing right. But if you show favoritism, you sin and are convicted by the law as lawbreakers. For whoever keeps the whole law and yet stumbles at just one point is guilty of breaking all of it. For he who said, "You shall not commit adultery," also said, "You shall not murder." If you do not commit adultery but do commit murder, you have become a lawbreaker.

Speak and act as those who are going to be judged by the law that gives freedom, because judgment without mercy will be shown to anyone who has not been merciful. Mercy triumphs over judgment.

What good is it, my brothers and sisters, if someone claims to have faith but has no deeds? Can such faith save them? Suppose a brother or a sister is without clothes and daily food. If one of you says to them, "Go in peace; keep warm and well fed," but does nothing about their physical needs, what good is it? In the same way, faith by itself, if it is not accompanied by action, is dead.

What are the salient points for us?

1. We should treat both rich and poor alike.

2. "Love your neighbor as yourself" (Leviticus 19:18) is here applied to the less materially blessed—in the Luke 10 (Good Samaritan) sense.

3. We may be doing everything else right, but if we are discriminating against the poor, or not loving them as ourselves, we are convicted as lawbreakers. Let us reword the challenge: If you do share your faith but do not care about the poor, you have become a lawbreaker. Is this a hard teaching?

4. Actively loving our less wealthy neighbors (showing mercy) is the attitude we should have if we expect God to be merciful towards us.

5. "Keep warm and well fed..." is not just an illustration to show the necessity of faith and deeds. Yet is this not what we are in effect saying to millions of neighbors the world over? (and many of them are fellow believers).

James' final remarks about rich/poor are in 5:1-6. His critiques of the rich: *"You have lived on earth in luxury and self-indulgence"* (5a). Is this the position many Western Christians are in?

Summary

We have studied enough Scripture to see that God expects his people to take care of the poor. In every major section of God's word—law, prophets, writings, gospels, acts, the letters—we see God's burning concern for the needy and his yearning that his people will share his concern. Christ came to give us an example of God's desire. He helped the poor. His gospel is meant for all mankind. God expects this concern from Genesis to Revelation. He will insist on it forever, until the coming of the One who will reward virtue and redress all wrongs: the judgment.

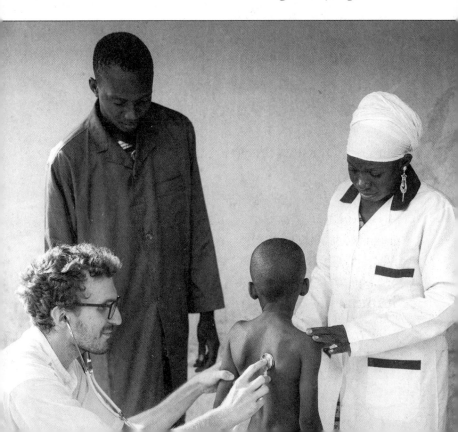

III. Dire Straits

Is the situation really all that drastic? After all, are not the impoverished of the world only an insignificant minority of the global population? Let us consider the facts.

The starving

There are hundreds of millions of starving men, women, and children in the world today. They long to eat the crumbs that fall from our tables and would gladly trade places with our well-fed dogs and cats. Many do not have daily water and are severely dehydrated. In fact, some 25,000 will die today because of inadequate food and related causes.

The malnourished

Out of our world population of almost eight billion, over six hundred and ninety million are undernourished. And because of inadequate medical attention, infant mortality rates are high; many will die prematurely from diseases that do not normally affect their well-fed counterparts. As a result of malnutrition, their minds are dulled, and their growth stunted. Life expectancy is far lower than the level we enjoy in the West. See the number of deaths per 1000 live births by selected countries below:

1.	Angola	205
2.	Afghanistan	184
3.	Liberia	138
4.	Somalia	113
5.	Chad	98
6.	Nigeria	94
7.	Sudan	92
8.	Republic of Congo	81
9.	Laos	77
10.	Pakistan	65
11.	Cambodia	54
12.	Kenya	54
13.	Bolivia	44
14.	South Africa	44
15.	Iran	35
16.	India	30
17.	Peru	28
18.	Vietnam	22
19.	Mexico	18
20.	Jamaica	15
21.	United States	6
22.	Taiwan	5
23.	Sweden	2
24.	Singapore	2

* Found at Infoplease.com.

The malnourished are generally not the ones who are brought to our attention, since photographs of them are less shocking than shots of the starving. The Parable of the Sheep and the Goats comes to mind as recorded in Matthew 25:35-36:

> *For I was hungry and you gave me something to eat, I was thirsty and you gave me something to drink, I was a stranger and you invited me in, I needed clothes and you clothed me, I was sick and you looked after me, I was in prison and you came to visit me.*

Or, in the words of the modern English poem, *I Was Hungry*:

You fed my food to your pigs,
you blamed it on the markets,
you blamed it on the Marxists.
You told me the poor were blessed.
You really did mean to write to your congressman.
You used me as a dumping ground
for your food mountain.
You promised to pray for me.
You were sure I could manage on welfare.
You switched the channel to avoid the sight of me.
You paid a pittance for my harvest.

You sold my government arms to keep me quiet.
You used my land to grow flowers for your table.
You told me to get lost.

(*I Was Hungry, an English poem, has been adapted for an American readership.)

The Sick

Diseases which we rarely encounter in the West, or against which we have been inoculated, are killers in developing countries. Medical attention is woefully inadequate in many developing nations, as was evident in the latest available statistics.

Physicians per 10,000 people

• Ethiopia	.03
• Chad	.04
• Nigeria	.38
• Jamaica	4.1
• South Africa	7.8
• India	8.6
• Iran	15.8
• Brazil	21.6
• Mexico	23.8
• United States	26.1
• United Kingdom	28.1
• Switzerland	43.0

The average Ethiopian would find it 65 times as difficult to make a doctor's appointment as a Brit and over 100 times as difficult as an American to access medical care today.

The sick and the poor are at our gate. But if we are to help to meet their physical and spiritual needs, we are going to have to act urgently—especially in countries where men and women die decades before they do in the affluent West.

In 2022, we summarized life expectancy in selected countries (numbers are rounded up).

Life Expectancy, 2022

- Chad 55
- Nigeria 55
- Somalia 58
- South Africa 64
- Ethiopia 64
- India 70
- North Korea 72
- Turkey 78
- United States 77
- United Kingdom 81
- Australia 83
- Singapore 84
- Japan 85

Conclusion

Some argue that there are too many people in serious need for our conversation and contribution really to count for anything. We might save a few, but we could never hope to change the situation of the majority, so why try at all? That is like saying that, since there are so many people drowning in the sea after the shipwreck, and we will never be able to rescue all of them, we should just let them drown. Moreover, the argument is not valid; if the prosperous nations shared their excess crops with the starving nations, everyone would have enough to eat. Ah, but that might have undesirable effects on the world economic situation. (Really?) Moreover, when medical technology and personnel are exported to the developing countries, hundreds of thousands and even millions can receive the medical attention they so desperately need. How many physicians are willing to forfeit their high salaries in Western practice for basic incomes in other parts of the world?

Considering the incredible amount of disease, malnutrition, and starvation; many, many of our world neighbors are indeed in "dire straits."

IV. Sisters of Sodom

The world situation certainly calls for action. Yet how easy it is, amid our abundant blessings, to become callous to the material needs of our fellow beings!

Amos 6:1a, 4–7 reads:

> *Woe to you who are complacent in Zion,*
> > *and to you who feel secure on Mount Samaria...*
> > *You lie on beds inlaid with ivory and lounge on your couches.*
> *You dine on choice lambs and fattened calves.*
> *You strum away on your harps like David*
> > *and improvise on musical instruments.*
> *You drink wine by the bowlful and use the finest lotions,*
> > *but you do not grieve over the ruin of Joseph.*
> *Therefore, you will be among the first to go into*
> *exile; your feasting and lounging will end.*

Archaeological research has shown that in 8th-century BC Israel there was an ever-widening gap between the rich and the poor, between the haves and have-nots. And as we deduce from the oracle above, people's lives in the time of Amos (c.750 BC) were consumed by such things as:

- High standard of living
- Fine possessions
- Rich food
- High culture
- Alcoholism
- Obsession with personal appearance

Their problem was not merely rampant materialism; they did not *"grieve over the ruin of Joseph."* In other words, they were virtually oblivious to the spiritual ruin of Israel. Today, awareness of the lostness of the world goes hand in hand with a concern for our neighbor's needs, both spiritual and physical.

God will call the affluent West to account.

Did not the people change their values, lifestyles, and treatment of the needy in response to Amos' sharp message? Not at all, which is largely why Israel was taken into Assyrian captivity (722 BC). Listen to Ezekiel's plea to Judah (c.590 BC) as he convicts them of their lack of concern for the poor. Ezekiel 16:49 reads:

"Now this was the sin of your sister Sodom: She

and her daughters were arrogant, overfed and unconcerned; they did not help the poor and needy."

What was the sin of Sodom? Homosexuality, adultery, murder, lying? NO! Her sin: she was being prideful, self-willed, individualistic, and aloof; she was overfed and unconcerned for the poor. In our casual acquaintance with Old Testament history and our somewhat artificial ranking of virtues and vices, we usually consider homosexuality to be a far more serious sin than aloofness from the hardships of others. Both are bad, but look how we have easily excused ourselves!

Perhaps through lack of knowledge of biblical teaching and facts about our relative wealth, we have become a sister of Sodom. It is tragic to realize that for many of us one of our greatest struggles is not to be "overfed." We struggle with our diet while the poor fight to keep fed. We struggle to keep up with fashion while they fight to keep warm. We struggle with our children's "higher education," while they fight to keep their children alive. Despite these incredible inequalities, less than one Christian in fifty give consistently to the poor in any significant way. The more aware we are of the desperate need of others, and the less we do, the more accountable we become.

Though our consciences may be clear, had we been on trial with Sodom, accused of her crimes, by our actions the same verdict would have been returned to us: GUILTY. Ignorance isn't an acceptable excuse!

Why is there a stubborn streak of "uncommitment" in some of our hearts that resents that verdict, and resists the message? Some Christians do not bother to attend midweek meetings; we do not expect them to enjoy a sermon on fellowship and the importance of attending all the services. Some Christians refuse to try to share their faith; it is understandable that they grow restless during a sermon on evangelism, or dismiss an admonition to serve and give to the poor. We must search our hearts, open our eyes— and the Bible—and pray for God to show his will, and move us to action.

Could it be that we have allowed our economic self-interest to distort our interpretation and application of Scripture?

V. Permission or Commission?

Part of our problem has been that we have seen giving to the poor as an option, an "extra." Some have even preached that we have permission to give to the poor but no command to do so, based on passages like Mark 14:7:

> *"The poor you will always have with you, and you can help them any time you want...."*

Such verses do not remove our obligation to help the poor. We *can* give to the poor any time we like. It is our decision *when* to give, not *whether* to give.

No commission to give to the poor? Nothing could be further from the truth! *"Sell your possessions and give to the poor"* (Luke 12:33). It is an indisputable directive from the Lord. Jesus himself was well known for his call to righteousness. His call to action regarding helping the poor was the acid test of a person's heart in the New Testament. With the rich young ruler, it was decisive, with Zacchaeus it prompted Jesus to announce the salvation of his soul, with Dorcas it was the thing singled out to inspire Peter to bring her back to life, and with Cornelius it was perhaps the deciding factor in God's selection of him as the first Gentile

to be offered forgiveness of sin (Mark 10:21, Luke 19:8,9, Acts 9:39, 10:4). Moreover, it was the only challenge given to Paul by the pillars of the church when he began his ministry. Giving to the poor is a vital part of walking as Jesus did.

VI. Sinners, Saints, and Samaritans

The question must then be asked, "To whom should I give?" There are traditionally two extremes: to everyone, all that you can give, or only to baptized believers of the Lord's church.

Giving to everyone is commonly referred to as the social gospel. Proponents of this view generally never gain much of an audience among our congregations because they discredit themselves by their imbalanced interpretation. The social gospel view focuses almost exclusively on meeting people's physical needs, a classic example of Christians making the same mistake that Martha made, which caused Jesus to say, *"Martha, Martha, you are worried and upset about many things, but only one thing is needed. Mary has chosen what is better, and it will not be taken from her"* (Luke 10:41,42). Certainly, Jesus came *"to preach good news to the poor"* (Luke 4:18), but he came primarily *"to seek and to save what was lost"* (Luke 19:10).

The other extreme, giving only to disciples, is equally wrong and biblically condemned. Many have held this position for years. It hinges on a rather

selective survey of the book of Acts as well as the narrowest possible interpretation of Matthew 25:40, where the "brothers of mine" are assumed to be the saved only. (Matthew 12:48-50 was a back-up verse!). Money is in chronic short supply and much needed to plant new congregations, so it would be a waste of the Lord's good money to throw it away to unbelievers, many of whom would probably never become Christians anyway (Matthew 7:6). These thoughts are inconsistent with God's power.

It is proposed that with the early church, benevolence was always an "in-house affair." But the astute Bible scholar also notes that Jesus never encouraged people to give to the poor among his followers but, as in the case of the rich young ruler, to go and give, then come and follow him. Had Jesus been interested in helping only his followers, he could have said, "Come, follow me and I'll help you to deal with all of that extra money." It was the attitude of "loving only your brothers" that Jesus corrected in the Sermon on the Mount.

Matthew 5:46-48 reads:

"If you love those who love you, what reward will you get? Are not even the tax collectors doing that? And if you greet only your brothers, what are

you doing more than others? Do not even pagans do that?? Be perfect, therefore, as your heavenly Father is perfect."

The loving heavenly father, father of all mankind though specifically of those who have come to Jesus Christ, causes his rain to fall on the righteous and the unrighteous (Matthew 5:45). This is the quality of love we are to have towards our neighbors, be they saved or unsaved. The whole world, we have seen in our discussion of the Parable of the Good Samaritan, is our "neighborhood."

We cannot afford to become so consumed in meeting physical needs that spiritual needs go unmet. Likewise, we cannot say that our neighbors are only our brothers and sisters. As usual, the Scriptures show us the proper balance between two potentially harmful extremes. Galatians 6:10 says:

"Therefore, as we have opportunity, let us do good to all people, especially to those who belong to the family of believers."

VII. London:
Repentance and Restoration

Up until October 1986, the London Church of Christ had taken up collections for Ethiopia, as have many congregations in the brotherhood. We had from time to time given to other benevolent works. But when it came to the area of selling our possessions and giving to the poor, we had yet to take the first step in restoring this New Testament teaching and practice.

After several weeks of intensive Bible study, prayer and discussion, the leadership of the London congregation concluded that it was time to put into practice what we had all agreed that the Scriptures taught. We resolved to repent, and as evangelists decided to lead the way by sacrificing clothing, sporting equipment, televisions, videos, stereos, silver and china. We challenged the congregation to join us for a day of selling our possessions for the poor.

The result was thrilling! That Sunday the stage was piled high with offerings to the Lord. Amazingly, instead of the sorrow that normally accompanies parting with something precious, there was a joy and excitement that defies description. It was like

Christmas in reverse, and the scripture proved true: Acts 20:35; *"It is more blessed to give than to receive."*

Our first concern was for our own brothers and sisters, so after the service we asked the less materially fortunate members to help themselves to anything they needed. We also gave cash to many members with special needs. The remainder of the clothing mountain was given to Oxfam for African Relief, and several brothers took charge of selling the more valuable items. In addition, a $3,000 cash contribution was given.

All the proceeds were given to the poor, to those within the congregation or those outside, through various charities. It was a beginning.

Where do we go from here? Sacrificial living and concern for the poor continue to be emphasized, and many brothers and sisters have taken serious steps towards a simpler lifestyle. But for the most part they began to channel their efforts into the 1988 Love Offering.

VIII. The Love Offering

(Editor's Note: We have included the story of "The Love Offering," because it was eventually transferred to HOPE worldwide.)

For many of us the idea of giving to the poor is appealing, but implementation is difficult. We live in an environment with very few poor people, and it is hard to be certain that our money given to charities will be spent wisely.

With this in mind, the leadership of the London Church of Christ have begun to organize a collection for the poor around the world. The collection has been dubbed the "LOVE Offering" (LOVE is an acronym for *Let Our Vision Expand*).

The money will be collected at the International Campus and Church Leaders' Conference to be held in London in 1988. The leaders or representatives from various churches will bring the offerings from their congregations and the money will be distributed immediately to strong churches around the world.

How will the money be spent?

The funds will help such things as children's schools in India and Africa, the homeless in South America, the oppressed in Soweto, the poor in Jamaica and Mexico City and many others around the world.

The Galatian principle will be applied (Galatians 6:10), which means that Christian and non-Christians alike will be helped, but the funds will not be used frivolously. Rather, whatever is collected will be disbursed at the discretion of leading brothers in strong churches (Acts 4:35).

Could any mistakes be made? Certainly, but then that is part of any pioneering effort, and Lord forbid that we should delay our obedience to this aspect of his will for fear of a few mistakes. Any area of Restoration history is bound to be characterized by a certain amount of fine tuning-if not outright experimentation. And who better to entrust our money to than mission-minded brothers who have sold their possessions to serve the poor around the world?

Is there any scriptural precedent? A good question, and an easy one to answer, since there are over fifty verses in the New Testament which deal with such a "love offering." As we have noted before, the prophet Agabus predicted that a severe famine would come over the entire Roman world (Acts 11:28). The Jewish historian Josephus recorded severe food shortages in the years 44-48 AD (Eusebius, *H.E.*

8.2, cp. Also, Tacitus and Dio Cassius), and Paul's eyes must have opened considerably when famine hit hard the mother church and all of Judea in 46. He immediately began collection plans for a contribution for the poor saints in Jerusalem, and it is much on his mind as we read through his letters (Romans 15:25-28, 1 Corinthians 16:1-4, 2 Corinthians 8:1-9, 2 Corinthians 9:15, Galatians 2:10). In the words of R. J. Sider (*Rich Christians in an Age of Hunger,* Hodder & Stoughton, 1977):

> Paul broadened the vision of economic sharing among the people of God in a dramatic way. He devoted a great deal of time to raising money for Jewish Christians among Gentile congregations. In the process he developed intrachurch assistance (within one local church) into interchurch sharing among all the scattered congregations of believers. (Excerpted with permission from the publisher.)

What about 1 Corinthians 16:1-4? Because of the controversy surrounding this passage, it seems best to cite it in full:

> *"Now about the collection for God's people: Do what I told the Galatian churches to do. On the*

first day of every week, each one of you should set aside a sum of money in keeping with his income, saving it up, so that when I come no collections will have to be made Then, when I arrive, I will give letters of introduction to the men you approve and send them with your gift to Jerusalem. If it seems advisable for me to go also, they will accompany me."

The traditional interpretation of this passage is that each Sunday a collection should be taken up in every congregation of the Lord's church. Many, if not most, brethren go on to say that the Sunday contribution is the *only* contribution that has "scriptural authority," But a closer inspection of the passage brings the traditional view into serious question:

1. The passage does not prove that there was a weekly collection. Instead, individual Christians are asked to save their money up, adding to their savings each week. The subject of the participle phrase "saving it up" (verse 2) is "each one of you."

2. If we are looking for a "pattern" for a regular Sunday contribution, we will not find it here. The contribution Paul is discussing is a *relief contribution*. How many congregations do you know who take up a weekly relief contribution?

3. The view that we ought not to collect money for those that aren't Christians must be challenged:

- Are we to assume that funds dispersed to the poor saints in Jerusalem were for Christians only? That is, if the husband were a disciple but the wife and children were not, would he benefit from the love offering while his family starved? Of course not. The funds were intended primarily for believers, but that does not mean that non-Christians could not benefit from the love offering.

- Normal Sunday contributions in most Churches of Christ support full-time workers in meeting the needs of the church. They cannot always predict whom they will be able to lead to the Lord and whom they will not. We sometimes set up studies with unbelievers who never make it to become disciples of Christ. Is the salary that supported this effort wasted? When we spend money on outreach to nonbelievers, are we spending funds righteously? What do you think?

- Many congregations assign a small part of their total budget to benevolence. The benevolence work is often directed towards both disciples and outsiders. Is this wrong? In what sense can it be said to be wrong for a congregation to do what an individual is allowed to do?

- In the light of all the Scripture we have considered in our study, there would seem to be no evidence that it is inherently wrong to assist an unbeliever financially, whether on an individual or church basis. Furthermore, we are not here advocating any super-congregational structure or hierarchy. No one has the right to *tell* Christians what to do that is not a matter of salvation (Romans 14:1). That Paul and possibly a few other brothers worked to collect the contribution from the various congregations involved in no way violated the essential "autonomy" of the local congregation. It was a freewill offering, and in 2 Corinthians 8:7, with apostolic authority and an apparent imperative to excel in the grace of giving, Paul carries on saying, *"I am not commanding you"* and *"Here is my advice"* in 2 Corinthian 8:8 and 10.

Thus, we see that there is no "authority" for the normal Sunday contribution in most of our congregations, and in fact there is no "authority" for *any* collection which is not for relief work.

We are not saying we should not take up collections to support full-time workers; that was done in the first century church, as is clear from 1 Corinthians 9:1-14, Galatians 6:6, and Philippians 4:14-19. Even our Lord received some contributions to support his ministry (Luke 8:3). Yet, ironically, the verse often used to invalidate a special contribution, 1 Corinthians 16:1,2, turns out not only to provide a precedent for a special needs contribution but provides no precedent for the weekly contribution many of us hold as acceptable worship.

Let us consider some principles to consider in discussion of a contribution:

1. Love of neighbor: This principle will allow considerable freedom for meeting spiritual as well as physical needs. Once again, physical needs are not more important than spiritual needs, nor are they on a par with them. But to neglect the physical in the name of the spiritual is an oversight.

2. Wise stewardship: The possessions we have been blessed with, including all our money, belong to God. For whatever purposes he requires them, we must be willing to let them go, for, in the words of Francis of Assisi, "It is in giving that we receive." We are mere stewards of that with which God has entrusted us. But we must not discharge it capriciously or frivolously, for God expects us to be conscientious stewards of all that he has given us (Matthew 25:14ff).

3. Expedience: If it is not forbidden in the Scriptures, either explicitly or in principle, we have no authority to forbid any matter of expediency. We have already seen that almost all congregations in our fellowship follow this principle in the Sunday contribution, which is not a matter of approved precedent, but one of expedience.

In case through all this discussion you the lost sight of the point of the LOVE offering, the 1988 LOVE Offering will be taken up to assist the poor, both sinners and saints, through the outreach of strong ministries around the world. This is a tremendous opportunity for you and your congregation to practically obey the command of Jesus to *"sell your possessions and give to the poor"* (Luke 12:33).

IX. But What about Missions?

"If we give money to the poor, we won't have any left for missions" is a concern expressed by some. As missionaries who often raise money for other missionaries we need to give to missions, our local needs, and the poor as well. The money we sacrifice could come from living and giving differently. When you were baptized and made Jesus Lord of your life, did you evaluate your spending patterns? Did they change? We are no longer spending money on sinful pleasures like drugs, alcohol, tobacco, parties, gambling, etc. The money we spent on these things now goes to the church. What are the radical decisions and sacrifices you have made? What changes in lifestyle that save money that you can give to the Lord and the poor and needy?

To meet the needs of world missions, the great commission (Matthew 28:16-20) and the poor and needy, we will need to spend less and give more money and time to the Lord. We need to realize the need and make changes in ourselves. Examine the permeation of the gospel statistics summarized in approximately 1985.

Frequency with which the average resident of

each continent might meet a member of our family of churches:

- North America   9 months
- Australia/Oceania   10 years
- Africa   40 years
- South America   100 years
- Europe   400 years
- Asia   800 years

Several years ago, at a major evangelism seminar, James Lloyd preached Ephesians 5:3-6:

> *"But among you there must not even be a hint of greed, because (this is) improper for God's holy people...For of this you can be sure: No greedy person—such a man is an idolater—has any inheritance in the kingdom of Christ and of God. Let no one deceive you with empty words, for because of such things God's wrath comes on those who are disobedient."*

Many disliked his message. Why? It teaches that we must examine our hearts for any trace of materialism. This is a hard teaching, yet many Western Christians take this part of God's word seriously. God's word is true. We need to grow in our understanding of God. As we do, we will give to God willingly.

Helping the poor will also help us to evangelize developing countries. Many countries place heavy entrance and residency restrictions on missionaries and other full-time Christian workers. However, helping their poor is welcomed. Several African countries and India take this stance. Visas are hard to obtain, many missionaries report. Missionaries have a reputation for being interested in the souls of the people, but not their economic and social welfare. Historically, convincing government officials of our interest in "the whole person" has not been our missionaries' strongest point. When restrictive governments see a broader, more biblical concern we can expect doors to open that otherwise may be closed.

We must see the world as God sees it and put the words into practice in our lives. It will mean growth and change for everyone. We will praise God when the poor disciples in the world outnumber the Western Christians of the world. Eternity with God is our goal. World evangelism and helping the needy was God's goal. Are you doing your part by using the resources God gave you? Let us come to terms with the fact that Jesus sacrificed and set us the righteous example that we should follow.

X. Where Do I Start?

If by this reading you see the need to make some major changes in respect to this area of Christian commitment, you will want to consider the following suggestions:

- Study the topic of money and wealth, biblically. Nothing is as personally motivating as your own study of the Bible.

- Share your convictions with others: brothers, sisters, ministers, everyone you know.

- Sell some of your possessions and give to the poor and missions.

- Make a budget and live by it. Decide what you need to live on and what you can give. Be disciplined.

- Examine your purchases and ask yourself some questions: 1) Do I really need it? 2) Would I buy it a month from now? 3) Can I buy it somewhere else for less? 4) Why am I buying it?

- Pray without ceasing and fast regularly. Praying for God to lead and help you understand what you can do will help all of us. Fasting will help you realize the desperate need of the poor. Jesus did both.

- Reduce your out-of-pocket expenses. Consider how you can do this. Do you need to wear trendy clothes? Do you really need that trinket?
- Share what you have with others. Grow in the gift of giving always.
- Plan gifts for the poor, missions, and money for the Church.

Conclusion

Our willingness to adjust our convictions and lifestyle are good indicators of our ability to follow Christ. Brothers and sisters, let us be people of the Bible. We must learn to live our life as Jesus did, for our fellow human beings. That is the way he taught us to live. 2 Corinthians 8:9 reads:

"For you know the grace of our Lord Jesus Christ, that though he was rich, yet for your sakes he became poor, so that you through his poverty might become rich."

In Matthew 10:8, it is said a different way. *"Freely you have received, freely give."*

Acknowledgements

This book is built upon earlier publications and the help of others.

- Douglas Arthur: *"A Light to London"* and "Selling Their Possessions and Goods," October –December 1986.
- Douglas Jacoby: "This Is a Hard Teaching" Biblical Discipleship Quarterly, July 1987.
- In 1987, at the Boston Evangelism Seminar, held in the Boston Garden, Douglas Arthur called the Kingdom of God, all disciples of Jesus, to put these scriptures into practice. All responded eagerly. God began to empower his church to help the needy worldwide and to witness his power and miracles through faith in him.

We are grateful to:

- *Rich Christians in an Age of Hunger* by Ronald Sider, 1977.
- Central London Church of Christ staff.
- Mark Templer, Evangelist, Bangalore, India, and his study on poverty in 1984-1985.
- James Lloyd, Evangelist, London Church of Christ, and his conviction on the simple life.
- Richard Whitehead and William Hogle, elders of the Crossroads Church of Christ.
- Crossroads Publications (led by Toney Mulhollan) for help making the original edition and to Illumination Publishers for helping make this revised edition available.
- And may all glory be to God.

HOPE *Worldwide*—The First Ten Years

Led by Bob and Pat Gempel. Program Cities Planted: 200. Nations Planted: 80. Population: 6 billion.

Goals by 2010: Continue our work in our focus areas (Health, Education, Children, and Seniors) by establishing the following in each World Sector:

- Volunteer opportunities—to meet the needs through Global Outreach and other programs.
- Hospitals & Clinics—to meet the needs of the medically underserved.
- Children's Villages provides small group homes for orphans and abandoned children. We will provide a caring "family," but we will also facilitate national and international adoptions.
- Family Centers—to provide resources and referrals that address the educational, social, and health needs of underserved communities.
- Senior Centers—to meet the needs of lonely or abandoned elderly.
- Computer Learning Centers—to bridge the digital divide between the poor and needy and universities worldwide.

Highlights from the first ten years:

- Established four areas of program focus (Health,

Education, Children, and Seniors), emphasizing volunteer opportunities.

- Received consultative status with the United Nations and registered with the U. S. Agency for International Development.
- HOPE for Kids (now Global Outreach) provided disciples with volunteer opportunities to help the poor and needy.
- Village of HOPE built to house families of leprosy patients in Delhi, India
- HOPE for Children placed 300 children with adoptive families.
- HOPE Youth Corps provided leadership training for hundreds of high school and college students.
- HOPE *Worldwide* Health Corps hosted professional medical conferences in Los Angeles, Jamaica, and Hong Kong.
- Sihanouk Hospital Center of HOPE opened in Cambodia.
- Sports Festivals hosted on behalf of thousands of orphans in Moscow.
- Family Centers/Orphanages opened in India, Indonesia & Romania.
- Senior Centers opened in Moscow, Berlin & Paris.
- HOPE Unity Award was given to Nelson Mandela, Mother Teresa, Jimmy and Rosalynn Carter, and the late King Hussein and Queen Noor of Jordan.

I Was Hungry, 2022

A few thoughts by Pat Gempel, the widow of Robert since 2019.

Dear Reader,

I was hungry for God and his direction since I was a teen when I first attended a church that taught God's Word. I embraced the Bible including Matthew 28:18-20, "All authority in heaven and on earth has been given to me. Therefore go and make disciples of all nations, baptizing them in the name of the father and of the Son and of the Holy Spirit, and teaching them to obey everything I have commanded you. And surely I am with you always, to the very end of the age." These words are easy to understand and hard to put into practice. God tries to teach us, and Satan, our enemy, tries to deceive us. Jesus came to show us how to live. As the years have passed, one trial and victory at a time, I have kept on learning.

"Since my youth, O God, you have taught me, and to this day I declare your marvelous deeds. Even when I am old and gray, do not forsake me, O God, till I declare your power to the next generation, you might to all who are to come" (Psalm 71:17-18). When you turn 80, you are officially "old and gray". I am there now, and God is still leading and I am praying that the next generation will embrace, through my example, the challenge of using his power to learn how to use your gifts to help others. I have found it is a building process. Our hard times teach us how to love and give eternity to others. God's love gives us a unique upward call.

This book and other actions summarized by Douglas Arthur and Douglas Jacoby resulted in the formation of HOPE *Worldwide* in 1991 by the International Churches of

Christ. We are learning together how to love God, Jesus, and the Holy Spirit more and more as we give to others. I would like to share one incident in Calcutta with Al and Gloria Baird in the early 1990s that helped us understand what we needed to learn about feeding the hungry. One sunny afternoon we visited Queen Victoria's palace in Calcutta. The grounds are beautiful, the monument imposing, and the palace is majestic. Since the palace wasn't open to the public that day, few people were around.

Suddenly a young girl appeared, seemingly out of nowhere. Her black eyes and hair sparkled in the sunlight as she handed us a card saying, "Please help me. I need money for food and cannot speak." As we looked at her, she opened her mouth and revealed that someone had cut out her tongue. A gruesome practice, done so that children can beg more effectively. Man is sinful, and God wants to teach us how to love one another and pass his teaching on and on and on. "He who is kind to the poor lends to the Lord, and he will reward him for what he has done" (Proverbs 19:17). You cannot out-give our God.

Please give your gifts to the poor, spiritually, emotionally and financially, from now until you meet God. We must provide HOPE to those around us by Honoring and obeying God; Offering our selves; Promoting and protecting the lost and the poor; Excelling in giving.

Love to all, Pat Gempel

Find ways to
give and serve at
www.hopeww.org